heartstrings and harmonies

Luke H. Snyder

For Milo Joseph Snyder

/forward

What started as a bunch of half-written songs and scattered thoughts turned into something bigger—a journey inward. These poems follow the path from messy feelings to something that finally makes a little more sense.

As I kept working through the words, a kind of rhythm showed up—not just in the writing, but in the way things started to make sense. What used to feel incomplete began to feel like part of a bigger picture. These poems tell that story—the ups and downs, the changes, the moments of clarity.

At the end of the day, creativity isn't just about expressing yourself—it's about figuring things out along the way. What you'll find in these pages isn't just writing; it's a piece of a soul, laid bare and unafraid.
Welcome to the unfolding.

Luke H. Snyder

/ *heartstrings and harmonies*

i promise to make you proud
even when the world pulls me down
i'm sorry for the distance
between our conversations
for the times i've seemed far away
the disappointment i see in your eyes
i never meant to cause you pain
the cycle of trouble wears you thin
i know i'm not always who you hope i'll be
and you love me wider than the mississippi
but just know
i'll never get tired of loving you
even if i don't always show it
even when life pulls me in a hundred directions
my heart is always with you
even when my mind is scattered
lost in the noise
i've been trying to find my way
but mama,
i've never stopped needing you
i'll find my way back to you
no matter how far i seem

/ *dear mama*

you were the first to show us
our youth isn't invincible
a lesson learned too soon

i still find myself daydreaming
for the days i'd catch a glimpse of you
in the halls
your presence so beautiful

i'll never understand
how fourteen years
since that october
have stretched
like a second lifetime
each season
your absence
still sits beside me

and the innocence
we buried
with you

/ *october 27*th

there's nothing wrong with me

or maybe there is

i struggle to hold a conversation
without the comfort of my foot
dragging back and forth

i throw in eye contact
to pretend i'm here
while the same song
plays on repeat in my mind

a dark-eyed junco
catches the last of my attention
while my left hand
fidgets with the ligaments of my right palm

/ adhd

in the early afternoon
i finally laid eyes on you—
so fragile
so pure

my son,
my heart bled into yours
in that moment
i kept our connection to your mother
for we will always share this bond

i promise to protect you
if you promise to save me from the dark
you didn't cry
you just looked into my soul
and with your first breath,
you connected with me

so clean
so beautiful
so magical
so perfect—
this world is yours to conquer

/ *milo joseph*

in the golden glow of the setting sun
i found you—
my future unfolding in your eyes

as twilight kissed the sky
we shared green tea shots
and i knew
you were my soulmate
my forever

through the despair
we rebuilt each other
you are my healer
my infinity

/ m.c.

i must have fallen asleep
in the early hours of
july 5th, 2021
and woke up sometime on
february 17th, 2024

/ coast life

i've spent too many nights
crying with no sleep
searching for healing
walking in the creek

maybe it's time to pack
my things and run away
find a new place
where i can begin again

/ *mass-penn*

i hope when it's all over
we'll find each other again
by nauset light
to the right

/ *nlb*

in those moments
when i wanted to raise my voice
it felt like you were a fugitive
darting through life
searching for truth

but deep down
all you really wanted
was the thrill of living
unbothered by the seriousness of it all

/ *chasing shadows*

i put my life on the back burner
tending to others
watching my dreams boil over

i miss the chase
of my own passions

but in this sacrifice
love grows deeper

and though i care for them
i am still nurturing the flame
waiting for the time
it can simmer again

/ let sit and simmer

stand
in the fire
of what we've made
watch
as our life burns
in the dark

the warmth has turned to ash
and our dreams are fading

stand
in the ruins
of what we built
each piece a memory
scattered
and shattered
a storm of doubt
tore this home apart
leaving our dreams
to fly away

/ *ashes to ashes*

when i strum my guitar
your memory fills the air

i wonder

when you touch his skin
do i cross your mind too

/ *red fender acoustic*

sitting on the back porch

lost in thought

i realize

it's been so long
since we danced beneath the moonlight

/phoenix jam

a black crow follows me
its shadow stretches across my path
i haven't named him yet
this constant presence in my mind

is he a sign of death
the reaper's call
or just a warning
of the pain that waits ahead

his silence feels heavy
i can't shake
a reminder
of all the burdens i carry
and the unknowns
that lie before me

/ *spirit animal*

you leave two pennies
wherever i turn
is this your way of speaking
guiding me with the shimmer of copper

/ *two coins*

breathing in the scents of home

each one brings a memory

i can almost feel
the sun on my skin again

/ *smell of gasoline in the morning*

some
days

it feels like i'm walking
through puddles with socks on

little irritations piling up
and all i want
is solid
dry ground
beneath me

/ chewing on water

misunderstood by those who only see you broken
they don't know you the way i do

they don't see the pain you hide
behind the walls you've built so high
or the kindness in your soul
that's never shown, never asked for

they don't know what you carry
or the dreams only known to the dark
only i know the fight in you
even when life has knocked you down
and still, you rise again

/ adam's not tall enough

for all those who fight their demons daily
i wish you strength
may you find peace
in the battles you face
and courage
in every step you take

/ down in a hole

be like the willow
strong in your weeping
standing tall through the years
make peace with the wind
let it lift you—just for a moment
embrace the sun and share your shade
winter will come, but don't be afraid
you will bloom again

just hold on until spring
let the mirror reflect
who you've always wanted to be
fill your wardrobe with dreams
you can be anyone

why hide your happiness?
why weep in silence?
the doctors may hurt to heal
are you afraid of their eyes?
don't wait for fall—
summer will return

dance with the wind
uncover your truth
show the world
what keeps you whole
and let them fall in love

/ strong like a willow

we're all different
but we're playing the same game
not the one on a board
where i always lose
but the real game
where every move
step
word
breath
matters

what is your purpose?
are you living
or just waiting
to die?

/existentialism

the world is crumbling
and you stay silent

i cry out to the mountains
but you don't listen

i hear children weeping
but you don't see

i taste blood in my mouth
but you don't feel it

the air is thick with burning
but you don't notice

i feel the hunger of millions
but you do nothing

/yahweh

i went to the cliff
wondering if i could jump
slipped on the rocks
and fell into the sea

i came home
seeking love
but missed their goodbye
now i'm unpacking boxes
from my childhood

death doesn't scare me
tell the devil to take my soul
to the bottom of the ocean
deeper than the mariana trench
where darkness turns to light

i saw my reflection
but it wasn't me
or anyone i knew

i wrote to you in my mind
the words so sweet
but no pen or paper
too dark to write

/ ode to the devil

i have been mistreated
like the leaves falling from the trees
the games we played were tied to my heart
i've been torn apart
split into pieces of a boy
who never understood why people break

someday i will listen
someday i will tell—
the difference between a drunken lie
and a sober life done right

what happens between me
and the devil below
is between me
and those who live in shameful doubt
i am a sinner
but others like me
laugh together
cry together
die together

i can't shake it
can't get it out of my hands
i love it too much
to let it go—
leave me by the bedside
until i'm drunk enough

/ *sins and a shadow*

her hand brushes mine
she apologizes
i sink back into the creaky chair
the smell of something burning fills the air

i place the burnt piece of toast on my plate
no butter, no jelly, no cream cheese
maybe just dip into the coffee

she sits across from me
tears rolling down her cheeks
on to the table
and i notice her packed bags
she wipes her face
leaves the missed strands of hair from her messy ponytail
i know what's coming

ticking of the grandfather clock
she grabs her bags
and heads for the door

i was already a half an hour late to work
before she sat down,
so i lie down on the couch
stare at the ceiling
the apartment quieter than ever
my stomach rumbling

back in the kitchen
there's only half a loaf of bread
i make toast again
catching it before it burns
but then i remember—

/ *no butter, no jelly, no cream cheese*

the fear of never wanting to go home
hovers over me
a reminder of what i might leave behind

the ache of connections never made
and places
that no longer feel like home

i also fear
dying alone in the wild
with no one to witness
my final breath

both fears intertwine
the pull of home
and the loneliness of the unknown
leaving me in restless limbo

/ *into the wild*

simple minds and complicated drinks
fill a smoky room
that feels like it's closing in
my thick, poisoned blood
mixes with spirits, water, and ice

i push past sobriety
on a cold, heavy day
"just one more and i'll go" i always say
thank you, johnnie, thank you, jim
thank you, jack, thank you, captain
thank you, jameson, thank you, gin
you're my only true friends

/ *drowning in cheap beer*

i'm headed back to oklahoma
where i lost my mind
i'll raise a glass in this dusty bar
to the lovers in my life:
one for the dancers
two for my mother
three for the friends who drifted away
four for the future
five for the past
and seventeen for myself

making my way to the interstate
living out of my old ford
chasing every neon sign
to distract me from my life:
one for the dancers
two for my mother
three for the friends who drifted away
four for the future
five for the past
and seventeen for myself

/ *every country song is about heartaches, beer and trucks*

i turn the page of my unfinished nightmare
searching for somewhere to rest
day and night i find solace
in the escape of my thoughts

i wash my hair
drenching my eyes
in the same dirty water
that raised me

blood stains the walls
scars mark us all
we search for an exit
with no one to call

in a haunted room memories stick
my family and friends never understood
why my face remained unchanged

the knives are sharp
the knots pulled tight
i hear there's clean water
where we're headed

the promised land
we'll never look back
never regret
dying to save our minds

/ *haunted*

drag me down to the creek,

                                        yet again

wash my spirit clean—cold water—drip me out sunflower

i crave you still

light the black fire in my head

this rushing creek could never be so silent,
                                my life follows the current to
the glass waterfall

i'll be back soon old friend don't you worry,
                                     i feel the pressure of
the sun on my face

/ *born again iv*

do you think the leaves feel
something as they change
or does it take so long
like it does for so many of us

do the trees mourn the emptiness
when the leaves have fallen
or do they only notice
what's missing when it's too late

/ *autumn*

was i foolish
or just lost in what we could be
maybe i ignored the signs
believing in love more than the truth

but despite the pain
i find a way to let it go
choosing to forgive
to release what was

in the end i see
holding onto anger only pulls me down
so i will take with me the lessons
and wish you peace on your way

/ we're all adults here

i hope you never feel
driving through four states
with excitement swelling in your chest
only to arrive at an empty apartment
where our photos still hang on the walls
no note to explain
my calls unanswered

i still see
you and your paramour
moving our memories out the door
leaving behind the dreams

/penn-mass

hummingbirds dart for nectar,
                            their dance fierce at dawn

the wooden chair creaks

coffee brews in the cabin

birds chirp—squirrels scavenge

morning dew glistens,
                            carrying the scent of autumn

a beauty to behold,
                            welcoming the day

/*gökatta*

i wish i could return
to the days of collecting cans
for pizza money
and drinking mountain dew
while we played the first Halo
all together
laughing in the dark
as the world outside faded
it was simpler then
our biggest worry
was who would get the most kills
and who would win the next round
we were just kids
floating on the high of those moments
no responsibility
only the thrill of friendship
and the glow of the screen
that felt like home

/ kory got the first xbox

what is it about death
that eats away at the living
makes us distant
unwilling to make friends
to hold on to family
to let love flow into the dark

but if i could
spend my life
casting my light
i'd greet death
with open arms

/ *with arms wide open*

how does love
bloom and wither
so easily
so often
in our lives
as if it was never meant to stay
and yet
how does love
root itself so deep
yet rise again
with every season
like a perennial bloom
never truly gone
always finding its way back

/ *annuals and perennials*

once vibrant
flowing with life
now silent
still
hidden
left behind
waiting
to be home again

/ *oxbow*

growing up in a small town
when someone leaves
it feels like
a piece of me
slips away too

/ *st. anthony's*

i sit here
sand slipping through my fingers
turning to glass
before it hits the ground
dripping through the floor
like old memories
vanishing
in the coolness of the cellar

/ *time in a bottle*

when you have the money
you're missing the time
always rushing
chasing what's on your mind

but when you take a breath
and savor the day
the money slips
further away

it's a constant fight
juggling work and joy
trying to stay whole

in the end
it's the moments we keep
not the cash we hold

/ *currency currently*

ruby red blood spills from your nose

your white sundress, kissed by lilies,
                                 holds the last glow of sunset

i watch as your lips turn blue

in this hour, our shadows find no light

i carry your stone-grey body,
                        to the riverbank where we first kissed

and down the current,
                             our shattered dreams drift away

/you used to be full of color

i feel the sun's warm embrace
the wind's gentle kiss
though change and decay will come
i am never alone

the world surrounds me
every flower
every tree
every bird in flight
sings a song just for me

every petal
every leaf
every feather in the breeze
dances alongside me

in this eternal spring
i am alive

/ *eternal spring*

i can't tell
if i need sleep's refuge
weed's escape
adderall's focus
or cough syrup's numbness
to make it through

/ ailment's are not the problem

i wonder
which mask
i'll wear today

/ *everyday is costume day*

i've been waiting so long

melting into this chair

tried to stand but the world spun
time slipping through my fingers

by and by the sunset fades
seasons shift into something new
by and by the sunrise comes
routines change with a different view

i've been here for ages
my thoughts melting in my mind
tried to change but was lost for words
watching my life drift away

/ *beverly louise*

the world does not hear me
but inside,
i carry wisdom
and kindness
seeking harmony
in every breath

/ *quietly humming*

waiting for you
to pull into the driveway
i watch the cars
go by
each one
makes me flinch

/ *where'd you go, i missed you so*

take me to the river

somewhere   far   away

it's too dark inside
and i cannot breathe

take me to the mountains

                              above
                    high
somewhere

it's the same damn thing
swept under the rug

/ *take me away*

the drugs are never cheap
and when reality claws back
it cuts like a knife

i remember those nights
believing we could disappear
into the dark
like ghosts

but when the veil lifted
our choices
suffocated us

those days
like a haunting song
of beauty we chased
now twisted into shadows
that swallow us whole

/ *listen up*

holding you close
or letting you go
memories twist
like tangled strings
around my heart
and my hands

/puppeteer

pleasant street to pearl street
the air thick with the scent of dried weed
arizona cans shaped into bowls
moldy couches
our makeshift haven
the porch filled with laughter
fighting with your older brother
those fast moving days of freshman year

/ *r.i.p max*

meet me where you used to live
where we shared our first kiss
where love sparked and faded
the walls spill
secrets we once breathed into each other
memories woven into every piece of furniture
i walk this path alone
lost in the grime

i'm tired of the changing seasons
each falling leaf feels like goodbye
spring's hope—
summer's warmth—
autumn's decay—
winter's chill wraps me in its loneliness

in that dim room
i ache for your ghost
to feel what we were
meet me in the ruins of what we tried to save
where love once bloomed
in the dark—
i search for your light
in this oppressive world

/ seasons change just like they always do

in the fading light
you search
the corners

you fix your gaze
on what could be
as memories
stare back from the dark

/ *bloody mary*

don't be the girl
digging through ashes
for something that burned
trapped
and chose to stay
stuck
but stayed anyway
watching love unravel
into a slow death
clawing at closed doors

/jessie's girl

this town is full of snakes
they've coiled themselves
around my heart

slithering

through my memories

tearing me apart

/ *wolf-snake*

i lost it all
by the river's edge

each drive past your sign
memories cold
like a sorrow tomorrow

the sun never shone
beneath skies of gray
trust turned to dust
love slipped away

old exit 36
i ache for the past
but the pain in my chest
will never leave

bells toll with time
autumn leaves fall
in this empty town
where dreams dissolve

rolling down the highway
each sign
reminds me of you

/ old exit 36

caught between the days that slipped away
and the ghosts that stay
what happened to us
a question unanswered
forgotten

yet like a weathered stump
i will remain
rooted

/ *redwood*

do you remember waking up beside me
those moments of pure bliss

everything felt
perfect

do you want to run away
with me
again
backwards to fix
the now

/ *deja-vu*

sitting here
on a saturday
staring at the walls again

thinking back
to when we were
together—mi amigo

the front porch
alexa—
play morgan wallen

that old bar
cheap smokes
let me take a hit—
and i'm out

/ *ole berg*

do i surround myself with honesty
or do they simply tolerate
the moments i'm present

/ *friends or foes*

i feel like i'm living on valet time
picked up
dropped off
places i don't remember
not knowing how i got there

/priority parking

the first friend i remember
we played with matchbox cars in the corner
of that old school on the base
where the walls were yellow and worn
and the air was thick with dust

the scorpio was in us—
always wild
always restless
your dad blamed our trouble on that
he never could quite figure us out
but we were thick as thieves
inseparable
so much so that some thought
we were more than just friends—
but we always knew
that one day we'd have to part

it was inevitable
like the seasons change
still—
no matter how far we went
the distance always pulled us back

we found our way to each other
again and again—

do you remember
riding our bikes through the cemetery gates
the wind in our hair
the world so big
yet somehow
it felt like we were the only ones alive

there was magic in those moments
before we knew life would make us grow up

before we knew how far we'd drift apart
but in those days
it was just you and me
and the sound of our tires
on the old cracked roads

/jake created himself

i've tripped and fell in the past
but still—
i gathered the broken
pieces of myself

you will find your way too
only this time
you'll have the full picture
as you piece yourself back together

/ *my son*

the sun slips into our home
revealing the dust we've stirred
showing us all the cracks we've missed
asking us to rebuild

it peeks through the dirty windows
inviting us to play
i fear the days
when it hides
crying behind the wool

we long to be farther south
to feel whole again
for the sun is life
feeding our souls

/ *mr. golden sun*

what if you could clear your mind
of all its clutter
and let new energy fill the space

for me
it feels like wrong thoughts
arrive at the wrong time
maybe it's my arrogance
or maybe my mind is just too full

/ *where is my mind*

i woke up
just as you slipped away
no scribbled excuse
not even a "take care"

your silhouette
never looked back
leaving me alone

empty bed

haunted

even ghosts say goodbye

/ no sleeping in

i didn't know
how hard it would be
to tame her wild heart
every time i think i'm close
i end up lost
in a cloud of dust

/ *wild horses*

ashmont street saved me
pulled me from the rubble
brought me back to life
the strum of your guitar
was the rhythm
that made my heart pulse again

we wouldn't be here
without those nights
without the hum of the city lights
when all i knew was dark

we keep doing amazing things
turning broken pieces
into something whole
turning shit to gold
with every laugh
every tear
every moment we've built

here's to hoping
we can do this forever
to keep making something beautiful
out of everything that wasn't
to keep holding onto each other
through it all
and never let go

/jonathan the tank

in your room
thoughts race
far from home
shadows hum in the corner
ghosts are here
they won't let you sleep
singing bittersweet songs of
heartstrings and harmonies

/ *a song for another day*

what are you running from

do you think you're getting far

look in your rearview

it's right there

staring back at you

what are you running from

do you think you've escaped

turn around

it's no longer just a memory

/rearviewmirror

find your salvation in me
my heart spills
into your cold hands
my warmth
sets fire to the stones in your mind
my embrace
turns every bone to dust
lose yourself in me

/ *cold hands warm heart*

every word you spoke
was a gust of wind
trying to push me off my path
but i found strength
in my own resolve
a confidence
growing with every step
i learned to tune out the noise
and listen only to the beat of my own heart

/ against the wind

you tried to speak over me
but your words couldn't change my course
i kept walking
unbothered
moving through life
just as i always have
with my own steady rhythm

/ *my own worst enemy*

in the wreckage
we will find our way

through the ashes
we will find our light

/ *embers*

like a wildfire across the plains
our love burns through the pouring rain
i see the flames dancing in our eyes

we found each other in a world on fire
came together with a burning desire
i feel the heat melting time

/ heat of the moment

there's a ghost in the valley
dancing with the pines

summer is fading fast
colder nights are slipping in

don't wait for morning
to say goodbye

/ *everything comes and goes with the wind*

you keep poking at me
but i stay silent
fearing what might spill out
what feelings i'm not ready to face

maybe i overthink
but i can't help
but admire the new version of you
and hope
we're both headed where we're meant
to be

/ underneath it all

i feel like i've only scratched the surface
but even a little of this man's life
makes the world feel right

he drinks wine by the bottle
yet can sit for hours
devouring a book cover to cover in one sitting

he's had the strangest jobs
but finds peace as an insurance adjuster
for him—
life isn't counted in dollars
but in moments that matter

i remember his stories
like the time he shot two deer with one bullet
just to save time
or when he punched a man through a window
just to catch his breath
he marvels at turkey vultures
calls them beautiful
and can hold a butterfly
while running a chop saw

i'll never forget the day we met
him on crutches with a broken foot
a memory that brings a smile to my heart
one i'll always treasure

/ *incredible mr. white*

my mind is double-sided tape
never able to rest
racing
running
spinning
shaping new realities
weaving alternate worlds

thoughts crash together
ideas burst open
dreams rise from fragments
visions unnamed

i am creating light
in the endless dark

/ *sticky business*

there is no shame
in asking for help
in unraveling your mistakes

there is nothing wrong
with reaching out
to someone who will hear
your atonement

/ *asking for forgiveness*

am i uneasy
because i am becoming who i need to be
or am i just afraid
of letting go of who i am today

why is it so hard
to embrace this change
when i haven't fully understood
the last one

the pages turn too fast
the words shift
into a new song

as the sun rises
my eyes close
lost in racing thoughts

i try to find the meaning
behind this melody
is it a ballad
or just another one hit wonder
pretending to be something more

/ i still haven't found what i'm looking for

your brown eyes
cut deep into my memories
my soul
my essence—
you flow through my veins
shocking me to my core

your skin
your hair
your lips—
intertwined with my bones
wrapped around my heart

/ *my brown eyed girl*

heal me
as i fall
my life rushing by
too fast to hold

can't you see
it's only me
my eyes
have been closed
for far too long

/ *bring me to life*

watching my son find joy
in the simplest things
reminds me
how often i underestimate the world
and how much beauty
there is in everything around us

/ *mr. mom*

your hand on my chest

a spark ignites

spreads to my neck

your eyes meet mine

chills race

down my spine

/ *medusa*

it used to take you
30 minutes to spike your hair every morning
you'd walk into school
looking like a porcupine with pride
like the world was yours
and you didn't care who saw
cannonballs in the pool
laughing until we couldn't breathe
turning into black and mild
and smirnoff nights
as we grew older
our innocence chipped away
and we learned the taste of escape
i still feel bad
for breaking your arm in middle school
when all i wanted was to protect you
and leaving you behind
in the haze of college
chasing a love that never knew how to stay
you deserved more from me
more than the silence i gave
more than my own mistakes
and i couldn't give you that
but i wish i could
i wish i could turn back time
and give you what you needed
because you deserved it
and i couldn't see it then

/ ryan's a good man

i need a sunny day

a break from the rain
to clear my mind
and breathe in fresh air

i want open spaces

where the sun touches my skin first
a moment of peace
to start again

/ here comes the sun

help me grasp

my weaknesses

understand my mind

and the ache of lost friends

guide me through

the road ahead

through my troubles

my sins

and the battles within

/ *weatherman*

i walk these dusty trails
searching
for the peace
that's missing

i sleep beneath the sky
to find comfort in the wild
and rest my soul

by the fire—
i sit
warming my hands
letting memories dance in the flames

i fill my body with berries and trail mix
feeding myself what i need

i bathe in the river
letting the water remind me

i am alive

in nature—
i am enough

/ *the trekker*

i look in the mirror
who do i see
just another fool
staring back at me

i look into my eyes
who's looking back
just another joker
lost in the deck

/ *the joker*

at some point
the last leaf falls
autumn exhales
melanin fades to gray
and melancholy settles in

winter arrives
cold and unyielding
its icy grip suffocates the trees

in this shift
the world braces
for long frozen nights

/ *one last breath*

the dam has broken
emotions drown me

i can't catch my breath

i'm falling again
on your empty words

my mind is shattered
thoughts spill onto the floor

the pounding in my head

struggling to breathe
choking on your lies

clouded
i feel blind to everything
unable to escape

/ empty words

how many times have i cheated death
i won't know
until my time comes
all those moments i escaped his grasp
hiding from the glow of his scythe

do you hear me say i love you
do you feel me when i'm touching you
do you see me when they shine in your eyes
or have you sensed that it's your time

they say expect the unexpected
but it slices through
a phone that won't stop ringing in your head

/ *mia's song*

if i ever had a number one fan
it would be you
the one who's been there
since the very first joke
the one who's shared my loudest laughs
never needing an explanation
just knowing me
better than i know myself

you've seen me at my worst
and never flinched
you've picked me up
when the world knocked me down
without saying a word
you just show up
ready to ride
ready to fight

we've been through everything
the chaos
the calm
the dumb shit
and you're always down for the ride
no matter how wild
no matter how late the night
you're right there

through the years
we've built a bond
stronger than anything
that could try to break it
because no matter what
you've always had my back
and i will always have yours

/jd's always down

the crown of thorns on your head is heavy
searching for salvation
or am i just seeing another statue

beyond the mountain feels endless without your hand
weary traveler
or am i alone on this path

the cemetery gates rust with time
will i bleed
or will you stop the hurt

clouds vanish as they rise
high flyer
or will i learn to grow wings

/ *rust and wings*

there's a monkey on my back
i can't shake
twisting my thoughts
and turning every sound to ash

its claws sink into my collarbones
holding me still
it steals my crumbs
before i can eat

smells my breath
before i can breathe

wipes my tears
before they fall

erases my memories
as soon as i make them

this shadow is always near
too near
feeding off my pain
thriving on my fear
i fight
but its grip tightens
and escape feels impossible

/ *monkey business*

a bluebird perched on my windowsill
and for a moment
it felt like you had come back

the one thing i regret
is not holding on to those last days
when you were still here

i hope you know
i couldn't watch
my hero fade away

/ *blue jay*

i hope you hear the voices
of the ones who loved you
sharing stories at your favorite spot
laughter and memories
keeping your spirit alive
every drink they raise in your name
reminds us of the light you brought to our lives

/ *charlie pearl*

inside me
a crack deepens with every breath
am i ready to meet death—

i once thought i'd see beyond the hill
but now i drink red wine straight from the bottle

at the mouth of the cave
i peer into its blackness
three crows
dark as night

inside me
a fracture deepens—
am i ready to meet death

a shriek rips through
and i go deaf
numb to everything
i drink red wine straight from the bottle

the light ahead grows stronger—
it's time
the air thickens
my lungs fight for space
inside me
the fracture shatters

this must be what they all speak of
i suppose
the only way in
to paradise—
to kill or be killed
my bottle is empty now

/ i never confess my sins nor am i a saint

your surface is rusting
uncovering the truth beneath
the skin on your bones
revealing who you really are

let the ashes become wings
showing all you've survived

there is no turning back
from the nest your mind has built

your life was buried under ice
waiting for the sun
to melt

/ *emergence*

there is no closet
deep enough
to hide your skeletons

/ *karma*

if we ever lose our way
promise me
you won't stop
and wait for a sign
to come save us

/ breakdown

drop the fear
it never tells
the truth anyway

don't fold
even when
you don't know
where you are

/ *just keep swimming*

what has man done to you
you beautiful orb
digging
prying
tearing apart
the layers that once made you whole

what has man done to you
you radiant soul
weeping
flowing
your tears filling oceans
drowning your grace

what has man done to you
you sacred goddess
twisting
distorting
shaping you
into a hollow
godless shell

/ *mother nature*

deep dark depression
leaves its mark
when your mind is in the clouds
and your body is lost

the world keeps spinning
but you are stuck
it's hard to move
when grace has slipped away

listen closely
when i say
the pills you take
won't chase away the hurt inside
no matter how hard you try

a million lies
hide behind your eyes
and every time you step outside
no one sees the ghosts
you left trapped inside your home

/ acetaminophen

do you want to wake up far from here
it's breaking you
my love
but you'll be okay

do you want to leave it all behind
the chaos in your mind
you'll find your way
you'll see

/ *crazy life*

your heart of steel

floating away—
unbreakable—
impenetrable—
untouchable—
until—it shatters—

alone in the parking lot

drowning—(internally bleeding)

/ *heart of steel*

holding my breath......till it burns
thumbtacks...... in my fingertips
papercuts......on the webs of my toes
a lighter...... to the knuckle of my thumb
toothpicks...... between my teeth
a flashlight...... blinding my eyes
plucking......every last strand of hair

/ little things that make me feel real

give my eyes to the crows
let them feast on what i've seen—
the dreams
the secrets
watch them tear apart my nightmares

beak
         by
beak

carry
         away
                   my visions

/ eye for an eye

your voice
has finally
faded from my mind
maybe this
is what moving on feels like
letting go without realizing
until
...
...
...

/.........

i had your name
tattooed on my heart
but—
what hurt more
than the removal

was the one who held the knife
and carved it out
delicately
like the first slice of a wedding cake
i'll never get to taste

/ *icing on the cake*

apples to roses
a twist of nature
ripe and sweet
softening in the hands of time

monkeys to sheep
wildness to silence
one leaps with joy
the other drifts in sleep

self-driving cars
down a one-way street
no hands on the wheel
a future with nowhere to retreat

/ *where the wild things grow*

silly angel on my shoulder
won't you dance with me
and the devil tonight
our prayers and hopes
are fading
we'll burn when the flames
ignite

/ *dance with the devil*

beyond the moon
somewhere far
is where i long to be
not trapped in this spinning sphere
this boundless prison

or maybe
earth(here)sun
just drifting
letting gravity dance

/ *weightless*

i never thanked you
for being there for me
in ways you didn't even know
i know that's not us
we don't speak of our hearts
but i can see in the way you laugh
and the way you hold your silence
we both understand
the chaos of this life
without saying a word
the way we carry on
with our unspoken wounds
and our quiet victories
you know the weight i carry
without me needing to explain
and i know yours too
we don't need the words
to know what it means
to show up
to be here
to simply be
the world spins
we stand together
even when we're apart
our bond isn't in the feelings
it's in the knowing
of what it's like
to live and breathe
without the need for confession
because we see each other
in the space between
the lines we never speak

/ the hues of dan

you carry the hurt
i wear the shame

together

we set this storm

on fire

/ one and one makes three

a stranger waits in the woods
following me everywhere i go
just out of sight
but close enough

i feel him in the rooms
i feel him in the streets

/ *stranger in the woods*

i see the sun
through bare trees and pines
like it's peeking

through the blinds

never once does it tire

of seeing

old weary me

/ sundown

trace my outline
fill me in with your color

my eyes are wandering

bring me close—

steal my light
devour me whole

my heart is dancing—

shake my soul

/ *emotional impact*

sometimes
red flags turn to white
reaching out

what once warned me
has become a quiet plea for help

/ *signs*

we're headed for a crash

braced for the fall
but we keep sinking

deeper
        and
                deeper

it feels like we're walking through hell

/ *descending*

even in the pitch black
i see the silhouettes of trees
reminding me i am not alone—
or maybe
trapped here with them

do you think
they fear the dark too

/ *death valley*

wildflowers bend and break
as the wild horse runs
a heart too free
to be tamed

the sun dips behind the hills
while hooves turn the earth
racing the dawn

where the sky opens wide
the flowers follow
trailing in the dust

/ *spirit*

sing grace above the water
cleanse in the slow-moving stream
hum with the insects
breathe with the breeze
feel alone but safe
and remember why you are here

/ *current thoughts*

there is so much toxic waste
surrounding you
it's seeping
into our home

/ *toxicity*

my mind begs me to write
but my hands pull me to work
my legs no longer move
like they used to
and my feet burn on coals
my eyes weep from the smoke
while my heart grinds
searching for the love
i am worthy of

/ keep on keeping on

are you leaving me
in the cold to grow
surrounded by frost
yet still—
will I sow

alone in silence
will i rise through the chill
the biting winds
the harsh soil

leave me here—
i will wait for the thaw

/farmer's daughter

i feel trapped
though i don't know why

there is always
a door hidden
within these walls

/ *the unseen door*

nothing makes you feel smaller
than the jagged edges of fieldstone walls
rising from the earth
forming an invisible cage

the towering pines stretch
endlessly across the valley
water circles—
the shimmer
holding you in place

there is a force here
you cannot see
taste
smell
or touch
yet it binds everything—

the world finds its balance
and for a moment
so do you

/ *the smallest russian nesting doll in mother earth*

tiny trinkets on the window
rattle with the passing train
i just want to speak to you
without the world interrupting

leafless branches scrape the siding
in the restless wind
i just want to speak with you
without the noise

these little distractions
demand my attention
but darling
you don't understand

/ *silent lucidity*

your troubled seas are mine
but i am the one keeping you afloat
your dreams are mine
yet i hold you in bed
your desires are mine
but i try to spark the fire

/ shared dreams— one heart

walking barefoot on fire
hurts much less
when you are the one
holding my hand through the flames

/ *with you i'm immortal*

your voice is the wind
your eyes are my light
your hair—
pure essence
your body—
my world

/just getting started

if i could leave this body behind
travel back
to undo
the things i've broken
and return to make it whole—
with you

/ a million and more to be with you

a wise friend once said
"find a rock and build your house…"
you helped me lift the boulder off my back
and together
we laid the foundation
of our love

/ least of these

my heart pours like rain
calling your name
can you hear me
from your shelter
are you ready
to face the storm

/ *shelter me*

she's tangled in a past
she thought she'd escape by now
fighting shadows
that won't let her go
alone in her room
staring into the dark
wondering if you'll ever see her
or just leave another mark

she waits for a savior
but time moves too slow
each time she's with him
she searches for the strength to leave
her heart cracked by promises
chasing something that never answers

faith slipping like sand
she's prayed all she can
but you're still miles away
maybe she's already lost
maybe she's too scared to face the truth
if you don't show now
she won't have the strength to choose

where are you to save her
from the chains she can't break
caught in a web
of things she can't undo

/ *where are you to save her*

RuneScape and AIM messages
picking up the landline
only to be cut off
by the dial-up buzz
forget that—
it's noon on a summer Wednesday
grabbing a drink from the hose
then running to the park
kick the can until the Porter Street lights flicker on
then supper—chop suey
I try calling you on your Razor
but all I hear is Vivaldi's Spring
and silence
now it's push-to-talk
heading to the condos for a game of Manhunt
life was simple
life was good
in the summers

/ *you've got mail*

i don't know
if i'm drifting with the tide
or if the wet sand
is just showing me where to go
and i'm choosing to follow

/ *caught in the undertow*

sober trust has shattered,
                    now i bleed

each drop a distance i cannot outrun

empty promises feed the wound i feed

a quiet ache,
                    a blindness left undone

raw cuts pull me under with each dawn

while the world moves on,
                    i stay undone

/ *sestet #4*

you're my true soul brother
i miss the days
we ran wild
free—
wrecking havoc on the weeks of the 4th
those moments stuck on
endless replay in my mind

but time moves
we grow older
wiser?
still—
i'm sorry for the distance
but we'll be together soon

the belly laughs
the all night nonsense talks
the memories we made

i'm proud of who you're becoming
Hawkeye—
life takes us on paths we didn't plan
but by grace we make it through
and come out stronger

i wouldn't be who i am without you
i hope you know that

/ *live action colby*

the mark of the beast
has been chasing me
prodding my last nerve
like adam
but it's eve i seek
in every woman i've wronged
maybe that makes me the serpent
lurking in the wastelands

/741

are ghosts
just memories

of those left behind

trapped in the rooms
where they last rested

/ *if you have ghosts*

i am the captain of a ship

a black crow
returning to the edge of the map

the waters ahead uncharted
yet they feel familiar
like i've sailed them before
in another life

with each passing day
i draw closer to the unknown

will it be dark
or will the horizon stretch
guiding me toward the sunset
to follow the moon
back home

/ dark side of the moon

i wander through the woods
lost in my thoughts
the scent of pine fills the air
when the world was simpler
and peace lived

the rustle of leaves
like an old song
i pause as if the earth
is holding me

but something shifts
a heat i didn't notice at first
creeping
rising
closing in

oblivious to the danger
i feel how quickly things change
how easily the past fades
into something else

/ *forest fire*

i see the world
through shattered glass
that never quite fit together

time presses like a stone
in my chest
i can't remember
when i stopped feeling alive

the bottle's cracked
still holding something
choices
i never made
slip away in the glass

i see the scars
but don't feel the hurt
the bottle's empty now
but i keep staring
waiting for something to make sense

a reflection
that isn't mine

a life worn thin

i thought i could fix it
but now i know
it's too far gone

i drink to forget
but it all comes back
the bottle never lies
but it doesn't tell the truth either

through broken glass

i see the pieces of a life scattered
on the floor
i'm not looking for answers
just the cost of what's lost
every crack holds a part of me
but none of it is whole

/ empty bottles and brand new cars...oak tree you're in my way

ashes
carried by the brook's quiet song
each particle
slips
a ghost whispering goodbye

the current holds no memory
only a path
endless and smooth
soon the ashes merge with the river
lost in the pull
of something bigger

/ *umbagog on the catacunemaug*

i feel my body shift
small dark voids stirring inside
pulsing beads that slowly merge
thickening
retreating to the brain—
it walks on stilts in the numb

with each step
pins dig deeper
into places
i've never known

/ through the hollow

a raindrop on my skin
feels different
from the warmth of a shower

i find relief in the rain
nature washing me clean
becoming one
with the cycle

/ have you ever seen the rain

doors are opening
but i'm stuck in this chair
waiting

/ *waiting room*

how do i fill my days
with memories i can't keep
when i leave this place

i think of the moments
i thought would last forever—
the warmth of the sun
the sound of laughter
with friends no longer here
the comfort of old routines
that have slowly slipped away

how do i live a full life
in such little time

i wonder if i missed something
if there's more i should've done
more i should've said

but then i remember
the people who still make me smile
the memories I hold close
even as they fade

maybe that's enough

/ *life is good*

i must've been
astronomically wrong
thinking the world
revolved around me

the sun is always
in my eyes

i must've been
grammatically wrong
when my words
didn't match my thoughts

my mouth
always telling lies

/ *out in orbit*

the problems in my mind
feel like the end of the world
yet i am just a grain of sand
on a beach swept by tides
beneath the moon's pull

a speck of stardust
on a greater orb
floating, spinning
endlessly existing
in something unknown
unfathomably beautiful
unfathomably deep, dark,
distant, empty, full,
wide, untouched, unexplored
unexpected, mysterious

i wonder what would happen
if our vessel broke free
and drifted away from the sun
would we shelter ourselves
and wait for the freeze
or would we embrace the unexplained
a love unlike any other
a whole love
no more fighting when war no longer matters
no more land to conquer when only ashes remain

will we adapt—
brave the elements
learn that our ancestors
prepared us for the end
realize that scientists are just guessing
and no one knows a damn thing

if death is coming anyway

why not carry the light
into the darkness

/ *experience the universe*

if i speak in stars
i'd ask the sky
to change its temperature
just to see the moon

but if i stay grounded
i wouldn't change a thing
because with an eclipse
comes the cold

/ the wolf moon rises tonight

time moves
without asking permission
it slips through your fingers
and you wonder
where it went

/ *the harshest reality*

if i had eyes in the back of my head
would i see the chances i missed
the beauty i pass without knowing its worth
would i peer into the past
wishing to change my future
or get stuck there
wanting to turn back

if i had two hearts
would i love more wisely
able to pour one out
empty it like i always do
but knowing the other waits
untouched
for when i break

two brains wouldn't help
two wrongs always lead me in circles

maybe i could fix my two left feet
stop repeating the same steps
trapped in the same dance

and then i'd ask for new hands
ones that could take back what was stolen

let my spirit slip from this skin
free to fly

/ *second chances*

a shift so small at first
you don't feel it
until it's too late

each change so subtle
you barely notice
but they gather
grow
until you can no longer pretend

the world flips
the scales tip
irreversible
a new order takes root

no going back
no turning the tide
what seemed gentle
now a storm

it's the little things
the ones we ignore
that pile up
until the earth cracks
and we're left to face
all we let slip through our hands

/ *climate tipping point*

the outer form

is only a mirror

of the self

to touch

the depths inside

thoughts

        and

            dreams

search for their truth

/ float on

where there is water

there are always predators

be wary of those
who come uninvited

/ *true blood*

i never believed in giving flowers
a gift that wilts
a symbol of love
torn from its roots
to be held in your hands
only to die

these beautiful things
cut off from life
given to someone i love
and now it's their job
to keep them alive
until they surrender
to time's decay

i take the rose
its petals soft with promise
but i know
it will die by next week

so i offer it
saying "i love you"
but the truth is
the flowers are not eternal
but still
don't forget
i love you

/ kiss from a rose

clouds swirl thick with thought
lines of time stretch
open roads yet to be walked
onward we move toward what may be
before the new century calls us forward

/1999

the unseen arrives
when no one is watching
waiting
in the corners

believe in yourself
you're not crazy
just misunderstood
seeing what others cannot

/ the fourth kind

i remember drawing a fire truck
a simple red shape
a square with black circles for tires
a square window for the driver's side
a stick figure in a red hat
holding a hose
spraying blue water
onto a brown house
its four windows watching
a red door open
to the flames

the roof
chaos of red
orange
yellow
scribbles that burn

/ what i wanted to be when i grew up

when the flock runs out of food
they turn on each other
but i've seen the sacrifice—

one steps forward
bows its head
shows its weakness

it lets the others reach a place
they never thought they'd go—
pecking
pecking
until all that remains is red
pecking
pecking
until the feathers fall away

/ *chicken run*

does the moon chase the sun
around the earth
never quite close enough
but always burning when they meet
a dance of light and shadow
a touch that scorches
before they pull away

is it the sun's heat that burns the moon
or the distance that never closes
in that brief moment
when they align
does the sky hold its breath
or does time collapse

perhaps they chase each other
not in rivalry
but in a need
that can never be filled

/ the chase

they call it "cut a rug"
but my feet have been pacing
so long the floor beneath
feels like it's wearing thin

how long is too long
to wait for answers to life
how long is too long
to bury what hurts

why do I always wait
for the wrong time to be free

mentally—
i feel like
a hypochondriac
physically—
i am unseen
internally—
my soul
is slipping through cracks
externally—
my shell is breaking open

/you've got covid, next!

what if i've never truly slept
just closing my eyes
while my mind stays wide awake
eyes still searching
waiting for something to settle

        jumping
words

ready to
        spill

the noise never stops

i don't remember dreams
just the motion of closing my eyes
and opening them when they decide
like sleep is something i can't catch

when will i sleep
or have i been dreaming
all along

/insomnia

i wonder

what would happen if i broke the habit
would the spirit that's used me
as a vessel simply vanish
unseen by the change i've yet to notice

i've already forced out the demon of drink
but what if he still lurks
waiting to pounce
when i least expect

did he leave the day i said "no more"
or simply retreat into the dark

and since he's gone
i notice something else fading
the other spirit that clung
dwindling, decaying
withering in the absence of its counterpart

problems arise but where
where is the root
i don't know
everything hurts
and i've been numb for so long
my body's gone into shock—
numb to survive
but what's left of me after the fight

i fear the day i retire
when all of it
finally crushes me
when i wither away
unable to enjoy life
without the strings pulling me forward

i fear the day i stop eating candy
when the lack of sugar hits
and my body rebels
sending me into shock
a forced withdrawal from what i thought i controlled

the iced coffee
my constant companion
would i stay awake without it
what happens if i stop
would the lack of caffeine drag me into a haze
where i can't find the energy to rise

if i broke these habits
would i become a better version of myself
or lose the very essence of who i am
is this me
or just a mask
woven from the things
i can't bear to let go of
i wonder what would be left of me

/ large iced regular

poor bird
your journey south
interrupted—

no warmth
no sun

but don't worry
the north still holds its heat
plenty of time to rest

take flight in february
soon—your migration ticket will only need one punch

/ *injured goose*

leave me there
like a pile of dirty laundry
crushed in the corner
of the bathroom—
let me drown in the overflow
let the mildew seep into me

throw me in the wash
mask me with five different scents—
spin me through endless cycles
let me tear through your mind
when you least expect it
screaming
even when you don't hear

/ *wash, rinse, repeat*

if you walked away
could i follow your scent
or would you lead me to the water
and call off the search

/k-9

i could sit here for hours
maybe days

the sun can wait

"we needed this"

i whisper to myself
twisting my two left green thumbs

/ rain on a porch

i regret

letting the sweetness of honey
drift away

through the open sky

/ the bees knees

i wish
we all had the trust of a child
sitting in the backseat
eyes on the window
knowing
we'll get them there
safely

in their high chair
hands pounding the tray
believing
we'll feed them exactly what they need

when they sleep
thumb in mouth
trusting
we'll be there
when they wake

cradled in our arms
resting on our hips
counting on us
to guide them
with love and care

/ *trust of the innocence*

the world spins
too fast for me to hold
i reach for the moment
but it slips through my hands
caught in the clamor
i missed my chance to ride

/far behind

sitting by the phone
on another friday night
fingers tapping the screen
waiting for a call back

the clock ticks slow
each minute stretching into hours
i guess the reception's down
like my heart, like my mind
a signal lost in the static
like our words—

you must've gotten lost
in a world where i don't belong
while i sit here
staring at this glowing screen
hoping for something
hoping for a sign from you

/ *the waiting*

stuck on a crumbling sidewalk
watching pieces fall away beneath me
each step
pulling me further
from where i thought i'd be

/ *wrong turn to nowhere*

i run
but the past follows
knowing where i lost my way
it calls
and i still hold on

/ *deep purple*

would you forgive me
as we tumble
or would you reach for the nearest branch
and let me fall alone

/ *reaching out*

your roots run deep
through the core of you
but sometimes
you need a little love
to remind you
you're not alone
i will be the hands that hold you

i will give you the sun
the water
i won't let you wither
i will be the rain
that never forgets you

when life feels dry
and it's time to bloom
i will tend to you

i won't let you fade
not while i'm here
not while love lives between us

i promise to help you grow
when you need it most
to let you reach the sky

/ *my succulent*

your life feels
like a constant
toothache
throbbing beneath
the surface

you try to ignore it
but it grows
pulling you down
day by day

the pain digs deeper
into what's unhealed
waiting for someone
to make it stop

but healing takes time
and sometimes
you have to sit
with the ache
until it lets go

/ *tooth*

just once
i want to taste
the apple
just out of reach
to know the sweetness
that teases me
a world beyond
my grasp
but still
i wait
and wonder

/ *forbidden fruit*

oh sugar
i crave you so
give me more
of your sweetness
let it fill me
till i bleed
till my veins
tear open

/ the white lady

stand back from my ticking time bomb
i don't know when it'll explode
can't remember the last time it did
maybe the clock is broken
and the second hand stays winding
forever in place
tick
tick
tick
tick
tick
it will keep ticking
until it spirals back

/60 minutes

growing up
is realizing
the beauty in the bloom
but knowing
when to let it go
with gentle hands
pluck the petals
one by one
and watch them float
carried by the current
toward unknown shores
it is in the letting go
we find our freedom
it is in the release
we learn to grow

/ *love-me-nots*

i place my heart on display
so others can see
the paths they should not take

i give my mind away
so others learn
when it's time to leave

/ donations

do you ever look out at the ocean
and ask yourself
why you're still anchored
to the shore

/ beyond the pier

i miss waking up
to snow days
calling friends on the landline
running wild through town
as if school wasn't waiting
it feels like a dream i want when i sleep

now i dread the snow
its gloom
first fall is beautiful on the trees
but then comes the ice
freezing everything in place
locking me inside

maybe i'm just older
and can't bear the cold anymore
until the sun comes
melting it all

the muck disgusts me more
give me that dream
let me be young again
climbing snow piles with friends
at the train station
full of life and wonder

/ *snow day*

until first grade

i wore mittens everywhere
every season

now i wonder
was it to keep my hands clean
or protect them from the world
maybe it was just the way i was

eccentric and soft
until the gloves came off
and the rough edges showed
perhaps it's that
i don't know
where my hands should go
in conversations
so they're always holding something
or tucked away
or busy fiddling with the nothing in between

/ *"hey gloves"*

take the back way home
play a few more songs
let your thoughts wander
and do their magic

/ *therapy*

the rooster calls
for the hen
but the hen
needs no one

/ *two make a flock*

when will this roller coaster stop
the twists and turns
the rise and fall
the ache in my chest
and the thrill in my bones
the ride keeps going
without my consent
without my control
when will it end

/ *hands and feet in at all times*

i blinked and he turned one
time slipping through my fingers
i want to know him longer
to hold him in my arms
just a little more, just a little longer
feel his tiny heart beat against mine
but I know
one day he'll grow
wanting to run without me
to walk alone
and I wonder
will I be strong enough
to let go
or will my heart shatter
as his footsteps carry him farther
than I ever imagined

/ *the let go*

loosen your belt
and let your spirit fly
through the endless reach of the stars
i always find your eyes
where you pull me
into the night sky

are you the earth's protector
hunting bad spirits
as they crawl from their hiding places
you'll need more arrows
for all the predators slipping from their rocks

or are you the fool
stuck walking on water
your father poseidon's chains
blinded by the king of chios
for loving his daughter merope

forcing her to marry a mortal
her stars forever dimmed
is that why we've sent
countless apollos your way
still jealous of your love for artemis

while you battle the rising sun
just to see her again
only to be stabbed
by poison in your back
but who sent it
when you claimed to slain
every creature on mother earth

/ *orion*

amber glows on your skin
like the last kiss of the sun
red wine stains your lips
and in that smile—
the one i crave
as if we never left
the fire crackles softly
but my heart is louder
how i ache for the valley's edge
staring down at the ruins
we once emerged from
where we built and broke
and rebuilt again
now it's just us
alone—
let's shed our layers
and rebuild each other
from the inside out

/ lookout house

i guess it's always my fault
the love dies
because i get too comfortable
and my presence no longer excites
i give and give
until i'm emptied
and you never notice
until the emptiness shows
but i'm the one who's lost
the adventure
while you
are suffocating under pressure
and shackled
to the ship
you blew up
sank
and still think you're navigating

/ the giver

what hurts more than the words
is how quickly they left your mouth
like they had been waiting
for the moment to break me

/ *no take backs*

here comes the river
that old mighty river
i watch the water rise

here comes the devil
that sly old devil
hiding in disguise

it's a damn shame
feeling this way
i don't know
how we could ever change

here we go again
riding the storm
until the end

/ *reflections*

how many times can we say
we lost our way before we found it
who's to say we didn't know better
intoxicated words never held the truth

/ before we knew better

left town on highway 84
past new york
i knew then
i was gone for good

/ *south of the yankee line*

daddy's drinking again tonight
momma's burning through another pack
trying not to bleed as i bang my head
against the walls

i hear them fighting
the same words they shouted last night
the dog scratching at my door
i'm not the only one

this is every blue-collar family
the scars will shape you
into someone stronger
someone who knows how to survive

/ *family jewels*

when i was young
i thought i had it all
the power to fly
before the fall

but as the years passed
i saw how wrong i was
the mountain tops crumbled
life's too short to pause

yet one truth remained
as i listened for a sign
life surrounds us
and love will fill every line

/ take off my shoes and kick it

it's been raining every day
the sun refuses to touch my
melancholy smile
each word i try to speak
i feel
slipping away

i feel like i'm losing my mind again

my walls are shedding paint
to wear a fresh coat of change
my floorboards creak with the sound
of new beginnings
but i don't feel
quite as new
ragged and torn
frayed and bruised

my eyes burn with a clearer view
my mind spins with thoughts unhinged
but i don't feel
quite as new
ragged and torn
frayed and bruised

/ brand new

won't you shine a light
through the scars where hell
burned me raw
won't you cry your tears
so my dry eyes can
finally see
your love

/ bright

if flames could bloom into roses
i'd fill our bed with you
pick your thorns and petals
if you could live inside my heart
i'd pull it out
and lay with you just one more time

/gone away

changes, mixed blessings
now and forever
all love
locked away

in the rain
it was dark
hard to believe the good times were
stopped
gone

no one left
slipping away
planets in separate orbits

efforts made
but none of it mattered
thinking too long
and the urge to shout

it made wonder
someone had to be at fault

and that
was the hardest part

I couldn't help but notice

sinking somewhere south

obscurities only omen

short silent sobriety

/ *s.o.s*

can't seem to fall asleep
my eyes tremble with every blink
i scratch the sheets to occupy my hand
while the other presses softly into my eyes
to make sure they still know how to see

/ *too stoned to sleep*

is it the addiction
that makes my mind collide
or have the demons
finally found their way
into the spaces
beneath my skin
and now
i cannot escape
my head

/ *tapped*

you tore down every wall
so what's stopping you
from locking me in
with your love

/ *in jail*

an angler fish
rose from the abyss
for the first time
its eyes met a light
it did not create
and then it perished
was it seeking the end
or did something in the deep
urge it to rise
and warn us all

/ coast of tenerife

if only i had loved myself
this deeply
my whole life
maybe i would have been
whole

/ *empty shell*

how many have gazed upon you
from the covered bridge
never seeing your true form
never knowing the gift you hold

/ mulpus brook

i'm sorry for my absence
i was lost in my mind
trying to hold onto
what i thought i could understand

/ headspace

i walked a mile
in your shoes
but the path
felt like my own
with each step
i saw your world
and it was just
a reflection
of my own pain
repeated

/ *trying to understand you*

my son was sick all week
but all i could selfishly hold onto
were the moments of him resting in my arms
maddened by the thought
of when it will be the last time
i get to hold him like this

/ *sick as a dog*

if this was just a game
why did you stop
the chase
the hunt
why did you turn
did you tire of the pursuit
or did the fear of losing
make you retreat
into silence
as if it was never
a game worth playing

/ *on the hunt*

that familiar scent drifts in
like the wind through the pines
and i am caught
it carries with it
a whirlwind of past
and the sound of a time long gone
is it the memories
that burn deep in my chest
or the smoke

/ seminole wind

your sweetness
makes me ache
grows me
towards the forbidden

/ elderberry

cry me a river
while you drink the bottle dry
my tears fall
but you can't taste the salt
you sip on emptiness
and pretend you're full
but the love you seek
drowns in the space between us
i scream into the silence
but your ears are already gone
and when the bottle is empty
so are you
yet still you ask for more

/ another round

if you could listen
to the music our bodies make
you'd understand
it's like we were meant to harmonize
for the gods to hear

the way we move together
clashing, shifting through the air
the way we turn
moaning winds,
tickling wind chimes
outside our bedroom window

i feel your song
beating on my ribs
as you gasp for air
on my soulless chest
but i don't feel my body

you took me away
my lips still wet
from yours
but my throat so dry
reaching for the nearest drink
to soothe me

you're bad for me
but you're so damn right for me

/ *fruit wine*

what felt like five hours
was only two minutes
how can that be
i call out
but no sound escapes
i can't move
i'm paralyzed
all my senses fade
but the clock
is all i see

/ *vasovagal*

existential talks
religion and war
thoughts of abortion
polluting the shores

why do we have fingers and toes
two ears and eyeballs
but still can't forsake
the darkness inside

/ *theology*

there are always those little things
like a water heater bursting
in the middle of the night
shaking us from our dreams
when we least expect it
forcing us to face what we hoped to forget
a flood of cold reality

/ *water heater*

i feel like
i'm missing out
on so much
in my life
or maybe
i'm being saved
to truly
live it

/ lately

you stopped watering your flower
left it to wither
its petals turned brittle
and its roots retreated

you're not performing anymore
no dances from your soul
the world waits for you
but you remain hidden
below the frost level

your heart once bloomed
unfolding in love
wrapped in life
offering its colors, its light

you used to vine around everything
twisting through the spaces
between the sun and the earth
lighting up the darkest corners
but now you're still
waiting for the rain to come

ignite again
invite the sun
let yourself bloom
for you are made of stars
and flowers are meant to grow

/ *botany*

where do my good thoughts go
why do the bad ones
rise so easily
like buoys
they float back up
faster than i can drown them

/ *thoughts weigh heavy*

pull another card
twist my fate
bend me
til i question my faith
break me
So nothing is real
pull the secrets from the moon
with thread on a wheel
let it spin me
into the unknown
into something new
my future
with each falling card

/ the green witch

the river flows again,
                    fading into night

ice forms along its edges

only the summer sun,
                    can break its grip

the twists— the turns,
                    knot my stomach

oxbows, bridges, estuaries

each pass, lost downstream—
                    dammed

/sestet #5

let my sickness rise again
for within me, a fire is alive
i will create, untamed and bold
my plague will ignite the world
nothing can stop me now

/ *ace of wands*

they call it daylight savings
but nothing feels saved
i sit here
awake
wondering if it was ever mine to keep
the clock shifts
mind stays still
as the world falls into the lie
that time can be changed
we lose it
we chase it
we pretend it was real all along
but the hour
vanishes
and i am left with nothing
just a grain of sand
on my fingertip

/ spring forward:fall back

i find magic
in the ordinary
the plain
the overlooked
hidden
where nothing stands out

simple
yet so bold
no flavor
no style
yet it fills me
in ways
the extravagant never could

there is beauty
in the nothingness
unremarkable
savory
and sweet
all at once
softly
filling my heart

/ *vanilla wafers*

in the end
this chaos will soften
the struggles we carry
will make space
for lighter skies

/ *in the end*

i keep this card in my wallet
since the day we thought
it'd be a cool band name—
a joke, really, but one that stuck
a memory of who we were
before the world split

it's a cards against humanity card
with the words *becoming a blueberry*
a phrase that still makes me laugh
still makes me wonder
how we held on to anything
amid the chaos we loved

skipping class like it was art
lectures fading to white noise
while we schemed new ways
to cheat our way through a degree

not all of us played the fool,
some took it more seriously—
now off to better things
but for me—
and a few others—
every test felt like a game,
every paper a chance to keep the joke alive,
to prove we were smarter than the system

but the world outside was waiting,
patient and cold,
and one day it slipped in,
quietly, like an unnoticed storm,
and that's when the cracks started showing—
in us, in the dream we thought we could be

still, i carry this card,

this small, absurd piece of us,
reminding me of the days
before we had to grow up

/ *becoming a blueberry*

/ the end

Thank you for spending time with *Heartstrings and Harmonies*.

Every poem in these pages was written with honesty, reflection, and heart—and I hope something here found a home in you.

If this book moved you, please consider leaving a review on Amazon.

Your words help independent authors like me reach new readers.

Keep listening to the music within.

Luke H. Snyder

www.ingramcontent.com/pod-product-compliance
Lightning Source LLC
Chambersburg PA
CBHW030822090426
42737CB00009B/836